THE PILGRIM SPIRIT

Andrea Skevington

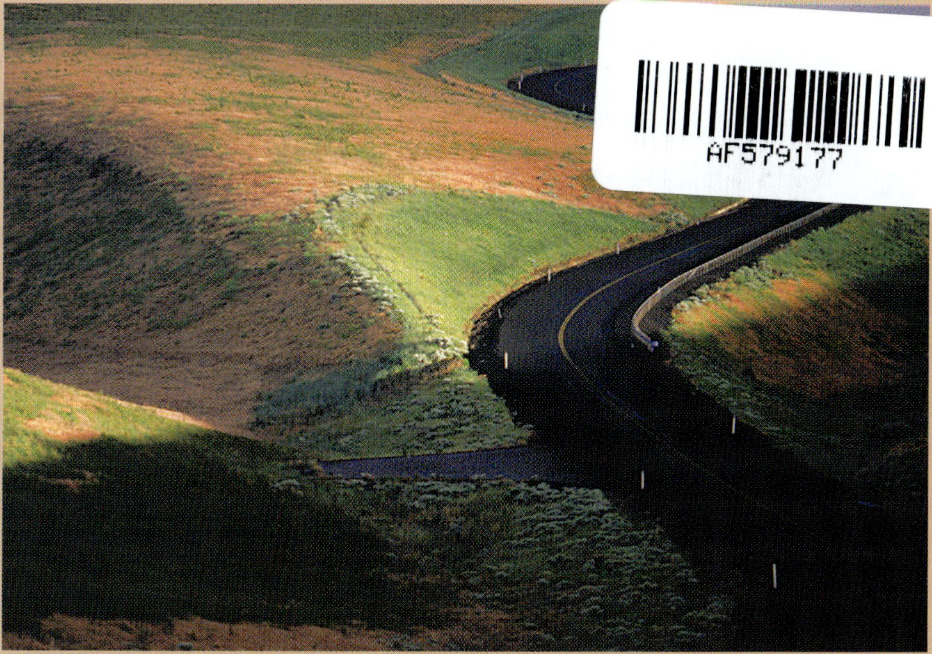

To Mum and Dad

Contents

Introduction 6

Setting Out 9

The Road 12

The Resting Place 17

The Pilgrim's Load 21

Transformation 25

The Valley of Shadows 29

Wild Places 34

Following the Footsteps 38

The Return 43

Introduction

A pilgrim is a wanderer with purpose.

PEACE PILGRIM

There are mornings when we wake, bleary-eyed, to the sound of the alarm clock, and struggle to find any joy with which to meet the dawning day. We pull back our curtains to gaze at the same, familiar scene, and long for a time when we leave our front door to go somewhere different. Our daily lives can seem predictable and

unfulfilling, and so some small part of us nudges us towards open horizons, towards that curve in the road as it twists through unknown hills.

> **I have no special talents.**
> **I am only passionately curious.**
> ALBERT EINSTEIN

This restlessness, this dissatisfaction, can be the beginning of something remarkable. Rather than dismissing it with a shrug of the shoulder, we could choose to listen to what our spirit is saying. We may be longing for a different kind of life, rather than

simply a change. We may be hungry for meaning, understanding and hope, as well as adventure.

Our spirit can be longing for pilgrimage – a journey into the unknown, but a journey with a destination, all the same.

> *Where there is no vision, the people perish.*
>
> PROVERBS 29:18

> **For light I go directly to the Source of light, not to any of the reflections.**
>
> PEACE PILGRIM

Our whole lives can be a pilgrimage, a journey of spiritual discovery. But there are also times when we need to travel with our feet, to walk through the world deliberately, with the purpose of allowing ourselves to be open – warmed by hope, guided by love.

> **What oxygen is to the lungs, such is hope to the meaning of life.**
>
> EMIL BRUNNER

> *Send forth your light and your truth,*
> *let them guide me;*
> *let them bring me to your holy mountain,*
> *to the place where you dwell.*
> *Then will I go to the altar of God,*
> *to God, my joy and my delight.*
>
> PSALM 43:3–4

Setting Out

Faith dares the soul to go further than you can see.
WILLIAM CLARKE

I find the great thing in this world is not so much where we stand, as in what direction we are moving: To reach the port of heaven, we must sail sometimes with the wind and sometimes against it, but we must sail, and not drift, nor lie at anchor.
OLIVER WENDELL HOLMES

Setting out into the unknown can be exciting, unsettling. It can prompt us to plan, study maps, talk to fellow travellers. But we know that however well we plan, the journey will surprise us. If it did not, we might even be disappointed.

When you set out on your journey to Ithaca,
pray that the road is long,
full of adventure, full of knowledge.

CONSTANTINE PETER CAVAFY

As we prepare, as we set out, we begin to shift our focus to our destination, and to feel its pull more and more acutely.

There is surely a piece of divinity in us,
something that was before the elements,
and owes no homage to the sun.

SIR THOMAS BROWNE

If I find in myself a desire which no experience in this world can satisfy, the most probable explanation is that I was made for another world.

C.S. LEWIS

Movement and growth are essential to life. Pilgrimage provides the opportunity for both, and the chance to explore a better way of living – fuller, richer and more open. Jesus said that he came to bring abundant and overflowing life. As we open the door and step out into the sunshine or the rain, we can choose to draw closer to that life.

Don't judge each day by the harvest you reap, but by the seeds you plant.

ROBERT LOUIS STEVENSON

That all things are
possible to him
who believes,
that they are less
difficult to him
who hopes,
that they are more
easy to him
who loves, and
still more easy to him
who perseveres in the
practice of these three
virtues.

BROTHER LAWRENCE

God provides the wind, but man must raise the sails.

ST AUGUSTINE

The Road

I learn by going where I have to go.
THEODORE ROETHKE

A pilgrimage that was begun in hope can soon be dulled by the weariness of the road. Sometimes, as we put one aching foot in front of the other, we simply long to reach the next milestone, the next stopping place. But, if we allow it, the journey itself can begin to work a transformation in us, quietly and gently.

I've learned... that everyone wants to live on top of the mountain, but all the happiness and growth occurs while you're climbing it.
ANDY ROONEY

I am a man of faith. My reliance is solely on God. One step is enough for me. The next step He will make clear to me when the time for it comes.

MAHATMA GANDHI

When I trust deeply that today God is truly with me and holds me safe in a divine embrace, guiding every one of my steps, I can let go of my anxious need to know how tomorrow will look, or what will happen next month or next year. I can be fully where I am and pay attention to the many signs of God's love within and around me.

HENRI NOUWEN

With time, we can become increasingly aware of our closeness to the world we travel through, learning the hard lesson of trusting in God for the next step. We can begin to travel with a deep, hopeful joy.

God is on the journey, too.

TERESA OF AVILA

As I walk,
as I walk,
the universe is walking with me.

FROM THE NAVAJO RAIN DANCE CEREMONY

The journey helps us realize that we do not travel alone, and as we sense God drawing alongside us on our path, we can also begin to align our steps with those of our Creator.

I run in the path of your commands,
for you have set my heart free.

PSALM 119:32

Jesus said to him, 'I am the way, and the truth,
and the life.'

JOHN 14:6

In recent years, many have rediscovered the Camino, the pilgrim roads to Santiago de Compostela in Spain. Their stories of the transforming power of the road have reminded many of the ancient wisdom of pilgrimage.

Maybe it's the simplicity of the life and the closeness to nature that makes one conscious of deeper realities and I hope, as a result, I have learned to be a better person, or at least I will try to be.

AN ENGLISH PILGRIM

To travel on foot is meditative and a recuperation for body and soul.

BRUNO KUNZ, A SANTIAGO PILGRIM

Your feet bring your private clay in touch with the ancient, mother clay from which you first emerged.

JOHN O'DONOHUE

Going on a pilgrimage is an antidote to our flat, prosaic, technical world. Mankind has always looked for paths where he can discover traces of the essence of life; to centre himself on a spiritual goal belongs to his humanity and gives his actions deeper meaning.

BRUNO KUNZ, A SANTIAGO PILGRIM

The pilgrim will also have the opportunity to show kindness without any thought of return. The pilgrim can learn to live openly, trustingly, with the transforming power of generous love, making the land they pass through a 'place of springs'.

Blessed are those whose strength is in you,
who have set their hearts on pilgrimage.
As they pass through the Valley of Baca,
they make it a place of springs;
the autumn rains also cover it with pools.
They go from strength to strength,
till each appears before God in Zion.

PSALM 84:5–7

There is no way to peace. Peace is the way.

A.J. MUSTE

It is within my power either to serve God or not to serve him. Serving him, I add to my own good and the good of the whole world. Not serving him, I forfeit my own good and deprive the world of that good, which was in my power to create.

LEO TOLSTOY

The Resting Place

Let me dwell in your
tent forever!
Let me take refuge
under the shelter of
your wings!
PSALM 61:4

We need times and places where we can pause in our pilgrimage. We need to rest and restore aching limbs, to renew our strength and energy. But we also need time to reflect. It is often at those times when we are doing nothing in particular, when we are emerging from our dreams, or when we simply stop, that we are surprised by insight, and suddenly see things clearly.

When Jacob awoke from his sleep, he thought, 'Surely the Lord is in this place, and I was not aware of it.'

GENESIS 28:16

They came to the edge of the village where they were headed. He [Jesus] acted as if he were going on but they pressed him: 'Stay and have supper with us. It's nearly evening; the day is done.' So he went in with them. And here is what happened: He sat down at the table with them. Taking the bread, he blessed and broke and gave it to them. At that moment, open-eyed, wide-eyed, they recognized him.

LUKE 24:28–31

Now is the dwelling place of God himself.

THOMAS R. KELLY

As I walked through the wilderness of this world, I lighted on a certain place where was a den, and I laid me down in that place to sleep: and as I slept, I dreamed a dream.

JOHN BUNYAN, *THE PILGRIM'S PROGRESS*

Cherish your visions and your dreams, as they are the children of your soul, the blueprints of your ultimate achievements.

NAPOLEON HILL

Faith is an oasis in the heart which will never be reached by the caravan of thinking.

KAHLIL GIBRAN

Along the old pilgrim roads many chapels were built, to allow the pilgrim time for reflection and prayer, as well as the opportunity to rest weary limbs. Such places often became destinations in their own right. One extraordinary modern example is the chapel Le Corbusier at Ronchamp, France. Its thick, curved walls are built with the stones of an earlier chapel, destroyed in the Second World War. Small windows pierce the walls, creating a diffuse, other-worldly light. Light also falls from the towers, drawing the eye upwards.

Important work happens within us when we stop, and allow ourselves to be open. Once again the pilgrim spirit will hold out open hands, and learn to receive.

As Jesus and his disciples were on their way, he came to a village where a woman named Martha opened her home to him. She had a sister called Mary, who sat at the Lord's feet listening to what he said. But Martha was distracted by all the preparations that had to be made. She came to him and asked, 'Lord, don't you care that my sister has left me to do the work by myself? Tell her to help me!'

'Martha, Martha,' the Lord answered, 'you are worried and upset about many things, but only one thing is needed. Mary has chosen what is better, and it will not be taken away from her.'

LUKE 10:38–42

Even as the water falls on dry tea leaves
and brings out their flavour,
so may your Spirit fall on us and renew us
so that we may bring refreshment and joy to others.

SRI LANKAN PRAYER

The Pilgrim's Load

I have held many things in my hands, and I have lost them all; but whatever I have placed in God's hands, that I still possess.

MARTIN LUTHER

Every increased possession loads us with new weariness.

JOHN RUSKIN

After some time on the road, we may be wondering if we were wise to pack so much. We may have begun to feel very differently about our possessions – for on a pilgrimage they become the load we must carry. We are constantly being told that we need this or that new thing in order to be happy. All too easily we put our trust in our belongings, not realizing the heavy price we may be paying.

The cost of a thing is the amount of what I call life which is required to be exchanged for it, immediately or in the long run.

HENRY DAVID THOREAU

I have learned to seek my happiness by limiting my desires, rather than attempting to satisfy them.

JOHN STUART MILLS

Once again, we learn from the traditional pilgrims, who travelled long distances on foot. They managed with little, and instead found other, abundant, sources of riches. Many carried a simple scallop shell – a symbol that their journey had a spiritual purpose, and a reminder of God's generosity.

> **Keep your hands open, and all the sands of the desert can pass through them. Close them, and all you can feel is a bit of grit.**
>
> TAISEN DESHIMARU

Much of Jesus' teaching was about money and possessions, and when he sent his twelve closest friends out to heal the sick and tell people about God's good news, he told them to take virtually nothing with them.

> *'Don't think you have to put on a fund-raising campaign before you start. You don't need a lot of equipment. You are*

the equipment, and all you need to keep that going is three meals a day. Travel light.'

MATTHEW 10:9–10

Sometimes, we think we will follow our dreams, or our calling, when we have the time and the resources. Jesus reminded his followers of God's generosity, and encouraged them to trust. He was very aware of the diverting power of possessions.

'Don't hoard treasure down here where it gets eaten by moths and corroded by rust or – worse! – stolen by burglars. Stockpile treasure in heaven, where it's safe from moth and rust and burglars. It's obvious, isn't it? The place where your treasure is, is the place you will most want to be, and end up being.'

MATTHEW 6:19–21

But there are other burdens we carry, burdens of guilt, pain and sorrow – like Christian's burden in *The Pilgrim's Progress*. With time, we can learn that these too can be given over to God, and laid down, so that we can begin to walk freely, and live joyfully.

> *So if the Son sets you free, you will be free indeed.*
>
> JOHN 8:36

Transformation

He who was seated on the throne said, 'I am making everything new!'
REVELATION 21:5

God is in the business of transforming lives – of making us new. For many centuries people went on pilgrimages in search of transformation. Sometimes, that transformation was physical – they were searching for healing. Sometimes, it was spiritual – they were looking for forgiveness. Pilgrims were hopeful that drawing closer to God would change them and make them new. The crowds who visit Lourdes, often at great personal cost, seek healing and restoration – and an end to their pain and suffering.

If, as Jesus taught us, God's kingdom is so close to us, why have so many people felt drawn to particular places in order to encounter God's transforming, healing love? The answer, in part, may lie in the shift in attitudes and focus that such a journey requires.

The Bible tells us of Naaman, who commanded the armies of Israel's enemies. He was a man of great power, but he could do nothing to free himself from leprosy. He took the advice of a serving girl, and went to see Elisha, Israel's prophet. He was not pleased with what he was told to do.

> *Elisha sent a messenger out to him with this message: 'Go and wash yourself seven times in the Jordan River. Then your skin will be restored, and you will be healed of leprosy.'*
>
> *But Naaman became angry and stalked away. '…Aren't the Abana River and Pharpar River of Damascus better than all the rivers of Israel put together? Why shouldn't I wash in them and be healed?' So Naaman turned and went away in a rage.*
>
> *But his officers tried to reason with him and said, 'Sir, if the prophet had told you to do some great thing, wouldn't you have done it? So you should certainly obey him when he says simply to go and wash and be cured!' So Naaman went down to the Jordan River and dipped himself seven times, as the man of God had instructed him. And his flesh became as healthy as a young child's, and he was healed!*
>
> 2 KINGS 5:12–14

Naaman had to step away from his own ways of thinking, as well as his own rivers. He had to learn to trust God for his healing. It's the same with the transforming power of God's forgiveness. Although it is available to us wherever we are, we may, like Christian in *The Pilgrim's Progress*, have to travel to find it. Christian had to leave his old life, his old companions and old habits, in order to reach the foot of the cross. It was only there that he was able to set down his heavy burden. Pilgrimage can have a key role in repentance, turning us away from those things we have done wrong. It has a practical wisdom, for destructive patterns of thinking and living can be hard to break if we stay where we are.

If we do not change our direction, we are likely to end up where we are headed.

CHINESE PROVERB

We are what we repeatedly do. Excellence, then, is not an act but a habit.

ARISTOTLE

O Christ, the Master Carpenter,
who at the last, through wood and nails,
purchased our whole salvation,
wield well your tools in the workshop of your world,
so that we who come rough-hewn to your bench
may here be fashioned to a truer beauty of your hand.

FROM THE IONA COMMUNITY

Be the change you want to see in the world.

MAHATMA GANDHI

The Valley of Shadows

Nurture strength of spirit to shield you in sudden misfortune. But do not distress yourself with dark imaginings. Many fears are born of fatigue and loneliness.

MAX EHRMANN

Every journey, and every life, will pass through dark places. We will have to learn to face the things we fear, and plot new routes when our road is blocked. We will need to think on our feet, and, sometimes, to walk into danger.

In medieval times, the pilgrimage to St David's in Wales was particularly hard. Thick forests echoed with the calls of wolves, and paths dwindled to nothing. There were stretches of marshland, high hills with deceptive passes, and weather that could close in suddenly.

The ancient wisdom of pilgrimage was that facing such dangers enlarged the spirit's capacity to endure, and taught reliance on God.

For peace of mind, we need to resign as general manager of the universe.

LARRY EISENBERG

The only true wisdom is in knowing you know nothing.

SOCRATES

'Fear not, for I have redeemed you;
I have summoned you by name; you are mine.
When you pass through the waters,
I will be with you;
and when you pass through the rivers,
they will not sweep over you.
When you walk through the fire,
you will not be burned;
the flames will not set you ablaze.'

ISAIAH 43:1–2

We can learn, through the practice of bringing difficulties before God in prayer, to put them in a better perspective. We can begin to move away from avoiding risk at all costs, and seeing monsters in every shadow, to a place of trust and hope. The mind's eye is powerful – the way we choose to see the world soon becomes the way the world is for us.

Fear makes the wolf bigger than he is.

GERMAN PROVERB

To the fearful eye, all is threatening.

JOHN O'DONOHUE

It is not because things are difficult that we do not dare; it is because we do not dare that they are difficult.

SENECA

Having dealt with the fear that lurks in the mind, we are better equipped to face the dark places on our journey.

God is burning out of you everything which is unlike himself.

MOTHER TERESA

Courage doesn't always roar. Sometimes courage is the quiet voice at the end of the day saying, 'I will try again tomorrow'.

MARY ANNE RADMACHER

Chance is always powerful. Let your hook be always cast; in the pool where you least expect it, there will be a fish.

OVID

As the rain hides the stars,
as the autumn mist hides the hills,
as the clouds veil the blue of the sky,
so the dark happenings of my lot
hide the shining of your face from me.

**Yet, if I may hold your hand in the darkness,
it is enough, since I know that,
though I may stumble in my going,
you do not fall.**

CELTIC PRAYER

Wild Places

Earth's crammed with heaven,
and every common bush afire with God:
But only he who sees takes off his shoes.
ELIZABETH BARRETT BROWNING

Sometimes our path will rise on to high ground. Here, vulnerable to the wind and the rain, the cold of the night and the loneliness of the day, we feel our own smallness, our insignificance. These feelings are the seeds from which wonder can grow. For if we raise our eyes, they will be filled with beauty.

When I consider your heavens,
the work of your fingers,
the moon and the stars,
which you have set in place,
what is man that you are mindful of him,
the son of man that you care for him?
PSALM 8:3–4

It is tempting to turn up our collars and rush through these blustery heights, eager to get to our destination. But if we do, we miss so much. The Celtic mystics sought out 'empty places', *Dyserth* in Welsh

or *Diseart* in Irish, where they believed the veil between the visible and invisible worlds was very thin. They believed it was possible to glimpse God, and the eternal. One such mystic was St Brynnac of Wales. He climbed the steep slopes of Carn Ingli, or Hill of the Angels, with its disorientating outcrops of rock. There, he saw visions. Today, when the mist lifts, pilgrims can still be seen seeking the presence of God. The Romantic poets also loved wild places, especially the Lake District, and their writing has encouraged generations to do the same. They believed passionately in the power of wild, natural beauty to restore and transform the spirit.

The farther I ascend from animated Nature, from men, and cattle, and the common birds of the woods, and fields, the greater becomes in me the Intensity of the feeling of Life.

S.T. COLERIDGE

Those who dwell among the beauties and mysteries of the Earth are never alone or weary of life.

RACHEL CARSON

Every now and again take a good look at something not made with hands – a mountain, a star, the turn of a stream. There will come to you wisdom and patience and solace and, above all, the assurance that you are not alone in the world.

SIDNEY LOVETT

My soul can find no staircase to Heaven unless it be through earth's loveliness.

MICHELANGELO

Nature is the direct expression of the divine imagination.
It is the most intimate reflection of God's sense of beauty.

JOHN O'DONOHUE

'But ask the animals, and they will teach you, or the birds of the air, and they will tell you; or speak to the earth, and it will teach you, or let the fish of the sea inform you. Which of all these does not know that the hand of the Lord has done this? In his hand is the life of every creature and the breath of all mankind.'

JOB 12:7–10

You are a child of the universe
no less than the trees and the stars;
you have a right to be here.

MAX EHRMANN

Following the Footsteps

Look where we will, some human heart has been before us with its offering.
WILLIAM WORDSWORTH

One of the joys of pilgrimage is a sense of unity you can feel not only with your fellow travellers, but also with those who have made the journey before you. You place your feet in the worn groove of ancient steps, or feel stone rubbed smooth under your hand, and know that many others have come this way before, seeking the same things that you seek.

You are here to kneel where prayer has been valid.
T.S. ELIOT

'I have loved to hear my Lord spoken of, and wherever I have seen the print of his shoe in the earth, there I have coveted to set my foot too.'

JOHN BUNYAN, *THE PILGRIM'S PROGRESS*

Helena, mother of the emperor Constantine, travelled to the Holy Land in search of the places where Jesus lived and died. She did this in sorrow for the wrongs her son had done, building churches at places touched by Jesus' life in order to bring faith and hope to others. She is known as the first pilgrim. And for the many who have come after her, setting their feet on the shores of Lake Galilee, there is the humbling knowledge that they, too, have walked where Jesus walked.

This intuition is present in all religions, which not only have sacred times, but also sacred spaces, where the encounter with God may be experienced more intensely than it would normally be.

FR FREDERIC MANNS

Many have found that visiting places at the heart of their faith provoked a jolt in understanding, and an acceleration of the transforming power of God's love in their lives. For some, it is an experience of pure joy.

She that sits on many waters, stilled waters, a blessed, pleasant land, replete with joy, may she sprout forth like the garden of God, and may she find the door of Eden.

ESHTORI HAPARCHI

On that day, I vowed that I and my family would live lives of joy, happiness, feasting and giving charity to the poor, until the end of time.

MAIMONIDES

A pilgrim taking this road will often end their journey in the bustle of a city – far removed from the tranquillity we often consider necessary for spiritual growth. Yet pilgrims who gather in the Easter crush of St Peter's square in Rome will be aware of the power of worshipping in the company of thousands. They are embraced by the arms of the church, symbolized by the curve of the colonnade, and drawn closer, perhaps, to their fellow pilgrims.

Important work can happen in the crucible of community.

As man draws nearer to the stars, why should he not also draw nearer to his neighbour?

LYNDON B. JOHNSON

We have flown the air like birds and swum the sea like fishes, but have yet to learn the simple act of walking the earth like brothers.

MARTIN LUTHER KING

Surprisingly for those who are used to the sprawl and isolation of contemporary cities, a city is a model for heaven in the book of Revelation – that extraordinary vision which ends the New Testament. The city, the new Jerusalem, symbolizes the peaceful living together of people with their God.

I saw Holy Jerusalem, new-created, descending resplendent out of Heaven, as ready for God as a bride for her husband. I heard a voice thunder from the Throne: 'Look! Look! God has moved into the neighbourhood, making his home with men and women! They're his people, he's their God. He'll wipe every tear from their eyes.'

REVELATION 21:2–3

There is plenty of room for you in my Father's home. If that weren't so, would I have told you that I'm on my way to get a room ready for you?

JOHN 14:2

The Return

The universe is full of magical things, patiently waiting for our wits to grow sharper.

EDEN PHILLPOTTS

Returning home can be a difficult business – especially if your journey has opened you up to new wonders, new insights. You can be afraid that all too soon you will slip back into your habitual ways, and thinking so, you do.

Perhaps, when we return, we could learn to look again – learn to be filled with wonder and joy at things that had become so familiar we hardly saw them any more.

We shall not cease from exploration
and the end of all our exploring
will be to arrive where we started
and know the place for the first time.

T.S. ELIOT

To be surprised, to wonder, is to begin to understand.

JOSE ORTEGA Y GASSET

What if we began to approach our everyday life in the same way we approached the journey? What if we decided to live by the pilgrim spirit and gently spread what we have learned to those we love?

The capacity for delight is the gift of paying attention.

JULIA CAMERON

Apprehend God in all things, for God is in all things. Every single creature is full of God and is a book about God. Every creature is a word of God. If I spent enough time with the tiniest creature – even a caterpillar – I would never have to prepare a sermon, so full of God is every creature.

MEISTER ECKHART

I would rather live in a world where my life is surrounded by mystery than live in a world so small that my mind could comprehend it.

HENRY EMERSON FOSDICK

Behind the façade of the familiar, strange things await us. This is true of our homes, the place where we live and, indeed, of those with whom we live.

JOHN O'DONOHUE

Every day can be an adventure. Every day can be offered up to God in the expectation that the God of the miraculous and the surprising will bring gifts to our door – gifts of people, of beauty, of laughter, of hope. For although we may travel to seek God, he is not far from any of us.

If I go up to the heavens, you are there;
if I make my bed in the depths, you are there.
If I rise on the wings of the dawn,
if I settle on the far side of the sea,
even there your hand will guide me,
your right hand will hold me fast.

PSALM 139:8–10

Find ecstasy in life; the mere sense of living is joy enough.

EMILY DICKINSON

Life is a promise; fulfil it.

MOTHER TERESA

For everything that lives is holy, life delights in life.

WILLIAM BLAKE

Perhaps, as we rediscover the joy of everyday things and delight in the love of those we have loved long, we will also begin to realize that we, too, are one of our Creator's great works of art.

People travel to wonder at the height of mountains, at the huge waves of the sea, at the long courses of rivers, at the vast compass of the ocean, at the circular motions of the stars; and they pass by themselves without wondering.

ST AUGUSTINE

We carry with us the wonders we seek without us.

SIR THOMAS BROWNE

The eye, when it opens, is like the dawn breaking in the night.

JOHN O'DONOHUE

Pilgrims leaving the holy island of Iona are sent on their way with the following blessing, which invites God into our ordinary, everyday lives.

May God, who is present in sunrise and nightfall,
and in the crossing of the sea,
guide your feet as you go.